Favourite Yorkshire Humour

collected from the "Dalesman"

1994

Dalesman Publishing Company Limited,
Stable Courtyard, Broughton Hall,
Skipton, North Yorkshire BD23 3AE

First Published 1992
This edition 1994
Text © 1994 Dalesman Publishing Company Ltd.

A British Library Cataloguing in Publication
record is available for this book

ISBN 1 85568 048 3

All rights reserved. This book must not be circulated in any form of binding or cover other than that in which it is published and without similar condition of this being imposed on the subsequent purchaser. No part of this publication may be reproduced, stored on a retrieval system or transmitted in any form, or by any means, electronic, mechanical, photocopying, recording or otherwise, without either prior permission in writing from the publisher or a licence permitting restricted copying. In the United Kingdom such licences are issued by the Copyright Licensing Agency, 90 Tottenham Court Road, London W1P 9HE.

Typeset by Lands Services, East Molesey, Surrey
Printed by B R Hubbard Ltd, Sheffield

Contents

Yorkshire Ways	5
Sporting Life	11
Hard at Work	17
Down on t'Farm	19
Queen's Highway	23
In Transit	29
Overheard on t'Bus	32
Market Days	34
A Class of their Own	37
The Age of Chivalry	41
Wedded Bliss	43
At the Coast	46
Church and Chapel	49
Hired Hands	55
Doctor in the House	58
Down at t'Local	60
Yorkshire Speyks	63

Yorkshire Ways

AN ARTIST WHO was visiting the Dales saw an old countryman whom he thought would make a good model. So he sent his wife to bring the man to paint him.

The old man hesitated. "Will he pay me well?" he asked.

"Oh, yes; he'll probably give you a couple of pounds."

Still the old man hesitated. He took off his shabby cap and scratched his head in perplexity.

"It's an easy way to earn a couple of pounds," the lady prompted.

"Oh, I know that," came the reply. "I was only wondering how I'd get the paint off afterwards."

A.D.

"WHY TED!" they said, as he entered a public bar of a Riccall inn, "thoo's 'ed all thi teeth oot. What's t'reason for that?"

"It's t'onny way they could stop me fra biting me nails," replied the poker-faced Ted.

L.M.

THE SMALL BUILDER took his friend over a house he had just completed. The friend was not enthusiastic.

"All right," said the builder, "you go into the next room, and listen." Then he called out, "Harry, can you hear me?"

"Yes," replied the friend.

"Can you see me, Harry?"

"No."

"Well – there's walls for you!"

D.G.

A YORKSHIRE farmer, visiting a cafe, was asked if he would have some trifle.

He replied: "Na, na, Ah wean't hev onny o' that – thur's ovver monny teastes at yance i' that."

P.R.

A SCHOOL PARTY had been to the village on a coach trip, and the talk in the local turned to modern life and education.

"Nay," said one old fellow in the corner, as he leaned over to a man who could have been years younger, "we make nowt of eddication up here, lad. We just uses our brains instead."

K.L.

TWO RAMBLERS WERE hot and very thirsty as they walked across the moors. They thankfully sighted a remote farm with the word "Teas" displayed on the front.

The farmer was standing by the gate as they approached. "Tea for four, please," they clamoured.

"Nay, we don't make teas."

"But it says that you do."

"That were t' chap as lived here afore."

"Oh! well, you must get it off before Easter and Whitsuntide or you'll be having a constant stream of enquiries."

"Ah know, we had last year and t' year afore."

F.N.R.

THE DALES FARMER'S wife looked across at her neighbour who had dropped in to see her. "Go ahead lass, an' hev another piece o' cake."

"No thanks," was the reply, "I've had three already."

"Tha's hed four," said the farmer's wife, "but you're welcome to another piece, lass."

J.C.

A MAN WAS moving house. He was warned that his new neighbour, a lady, was nosey. The man arrived with his furniture; he had just started to unload when the lady appeared and said: "Ah wadn't got inti that hoole, if ah wer yow; it's wick wi' fleas."

Said the man: "We've brought a teeam wi' us at'll whack em!"

H.W.D.

A DALES BUTCHER'S LAD was riding his carrier bicycle very fast down the street of the village, when he suddenly toppled over and crashed, sprawling over his machine and basket.

Passing villagers gave assistance. On being asked if he was all right, the lad replied: "Ah'm alreight – but Ah've lost me heart, me liver's mucky, and one of me kidneys has rolled down that drain."

T.S.

TWO MINERS were walking home on either side of a cobbled street. Joe noticed Tommy first.

Joe: "Is that Tommy?" Tommy: "Aye, is that Joe?"

An elderly lady watched from her doorstep and then turned to a friend, saying: "You'd think they'd know each other's names by now; they've lived next door to each other for nigh on twenty years!"

K.J.B.

IN PORTUGAL, I witnessed a display of Yorkshire pride. A Portuguese guide was extolling the bridge across the Tagus as the longest suspension bridge in Europe.

"Oh no, it isn't," chorused the Yorkshire tourists, "our Humber Bridge is the longest."

"How long is that, then?" queried the guide.

"We don't know, but ours is the longest," was the vehement reply.

The woman's English was not up to explaining the illogicality of their answer, so she countered: "The Japanese are starting what will be the longest suspension bridge in the world."

"It still won't be as long as ours," declared the Tykès.

The courier gave up – defeated.

M.B.

TWO MEN SAT at a table in a small Dales cafe. One was a burly individual, and the other a diminutive man in a bowler hat. They both concentrated on their meal for some minutes, when the little man tapped the other on the arm.

"Do you think you could pass the sugar?" he asked timidly.

The burly one scowled. "Ah reckon Ah could," he said, "Ah've been movin' pianners all me life."

L.P.

A FEATURE OF Yorkshire life was once the custom of children calling at Auntie's house about teatime, for a good tea was assured. A boy following the long custom called at his auntie's house and found two other visitors were present. When the time came "to draw up to the table", the boy was invited to say grace.

"You know," said Auntie, "like your mother does at home."

Each head was bowed and the grace came clearly. "For God's sake, go easy on the butter."

N.T.

IN A YORKSHIRE country village there once lived a vicar, his son and his grandson, and, as is often the custom in Yorkshire, each had been given the same Christian name so that there were three generations of John there. The vicar's harassed wife one day answered the telephone with: "Which one of them do you wish to speak to – John the father, John the son, or John the holy terror?"

L.T.J.

A DALES FARMER once put through a phone call and asked the operator for "one-nuthin'-nought-nowt". It spoke well of the local exchange that he got the number 1000.

D.L.

MEMBERS OF the village youth club went for a holiday to Gottingen, Germany. The visit was arranged on an exchange basis and the youth club members were to stay in the homes of teachers who had been given reciprocal hospitality in England.

On nearing Gottingen and while preparing to leave the train, one of the youths remarked: "Well, Ah 'opes ma 'ost kon speaak English."

"Aye," said his companion, "Ah 'opes 'e kon, cos thoo can't."

A.S.

"Look – a lesser spotted woodpecker!"

IN A LITTLE Dales town an evening class was studying German. "Now," said the German-born teacher, "tonight ve vill talk about a railvay journey: ve vill start on ze station. Ze German for railvay station is 'der Bahnhof'. Can anyone find a gut vay to remember der Bahnhof?"

"Aye lad, Ah can," said a voice.

Everyone gasped. It was the dunce of the class who had answered.

"Oh yes, Mr. X, and just how vill you remember zis vord – zis Bahnhof?"

"Well," said the student, "whenever Ah go to t'station, Ah'm allus bahn off somewheer."

The teacher never understood why the whole class roared with laughter.

P.J.

ON A VISIT to Castleton, in North Yorkshire, my husband and I attended the local show. Young horse riders were displaying their prowess over the jumps. As one young man approached an awkward jump, his horse seemed to hesitate.

Loud and clear over the loudspeaker system came the remark, in broad dialect: "Come on, John – never let it be said thee mother bred a jibber."

G. Atkinson

HEARING THAT a man in a Yorkshire village had reached the age of 100, the reporter interviewed a neighbour on the subject.
"You must be very proud of him," he remarked. "Oh, I don't know," was the unexpected reply. "The only thing he's ever done is grow old, and he's taken a mighty long time over that."

H.R.

HIGH WINDS had interfered with telephone reception all week. "Hello, hello," a woman shouted. "Hello, I'm sorry, but I can't hear you. The line is bad. Hello, hello, hello. What's that you say? No, I'm sorry I can't hear you. Hang on a second, I'll just put my other glasses on."

K.J.B.

I REMEMBER one day when in the Grosmont-Egton district I stopped my car on a steep hill to ask an old lady at her garden gate: "Is this hill dangerous?" "Not here, it isn't," was the reply, "it's doon at t'bottom where they all kills thersens."

Florence Hopper

ASK A BILSDALE man about the weather, and he'll tell you straight: "There's nobbut two soorts o' weather, good and bad."
On a fine day, he'll remark: "We can do wi' this an' better." On a bad day, he'll say: "It'll git worse afore it gits better."
Farming talk usually takes the same pessimistic view.
"How's taties, Joe?"
"Oh why, they cad do wi some rain."
Same day: "How's t' hay, Ted?"
"Why, it wants some yat sun on it, and then it's not as good as last year's crop."

K.G.C.

AN OLD MAN from Hawes paid his first visit to London, and stood outside Westminster Abbey watching traffic.
A policeman said to him: "Busy, isn't it?" To which the old man replied: "Aye, there's a trip in frae Hawes!"

Sporting Life

A FEW YEARS AGO, I was walking across Aireville Park, Skipton, and noticed a chap practising golfing drives. Sensibly, to save himself a lot of walking, he was using a couple of dozen balls. As our paths crossed, he had produced a plastic bag and was collecting the golf balls prior to the next session, so I nodded in a friendly way and grinned, "Fine crop".

His face remained quite serious as he scanned the heavens and tested the wind with a moistened finger. "Aye," he replied, "it's this warm weather – it does bring them on nicely!"

Wilf Proctor

THE RUGBY MATCH between traditionally rival teams in Yorkshire had reached a critical stage, with the scores equal and each side trying ferociously to gain an advantage. Several players had already been carried off, and several more had their jerseys ripped, when a particularly strong kick by one of the fullbacks sent the ball right out of the ground. The players hesitated, wondering what was to happen next. They were spurred on to further violence by a voice from the crowd: "Never mind t'ball lads, get on with t'game."

Lee Vincent

A YORKSHIRE FARMER had taken two wickets in succession with the last two balls of an over. As the fielders were changing over, a youngster ran on to the field and reported to the farmer that one of his cows was calving. With the chance of a hat trick, he carried on playing cricket, accomplished his hat trick and left the field (captain's permission, of course) to attend to his "increase".

Ron Yeomans

TWO YEARS AGO I was playing cricket for my local side in an away match at a neighbouring village. In the first four balls, 'their' umpire disallowed two lbw appeals by our opening fast bowler, who is also our captain. Hitching his trousers for the task ahead, he bellowed out in a voice which could be heard back in our own village: "Right, lads. We'll get nowt here. We'll just have to bowl this lot out."

Harry Mead

MY LITTLE granddaughter has been watching cricket all her four years. Last summer she was with her mother when the open golf tournament was being shown on television. She was watching so closely that her mother said: "Do you like golf, Joanna?"

Joanna said, rather unsurely: "Yes, but that birdie hasn't come out of the hole yet."

F.M.S.

AT A COUNTY cricket match at Headingley, a Warwickshire batsman trounced the Yorkshire bowling to the extent of even hitting the ball to the boundary with one hand only. "Bah gum, lad," said one hardbitten Yorkshire spectator to his friend, "yon beggar's played afoor."

Rev. John Stephenson

MANY YEARS AGO a man was passing a little country railway station on a hot summer afternoon. The place was deserted, except for the stationmaster and porter, who were having a game of cricket on the platform. The stationmaster was batting and clouting the ball all over the place. Try as he would, the porter could not bowl him out.

After watching this one-sided game for a while, the man went over to the porter and said: "Do you mind if I have a go?" He took the ball and bowled the stationmaster out first ball.

The porter grabbed him by the hand. There were tears of gratitude in his eyes. "Ee, lad," he said, "I'm reight glad tha did that – he's bin in fower years."

Roland Lindup

A LAD from the East Riding wanted to take riding lessons. He went to a riding school and was shown the horse, which he mounted.

The lively horse bucked, jumped and dashed about in an attempt to dislodge the young man. He hung on to the horse for several moments and then, looking down, saw the animal had a hind leg fast in the stirrup.

The lad shouted: " Hod on a minute; if thoo's getting on, I'se getting off!"

J. Digby Cooke

A SMALL BOY, newly arrived in the village, asked a local youth if there was any fishing nearby. "Aye lad, there's a pond in t'wood." The lad rushed off, found the pond, giving but a glance at the sign which, had be been able to read, said "No Fishing".

His concentration on angling was soon shattered when an irate voice roared in his ear: "Can't tha read what it says on t'sign, lad – it says no fishin'." Taken aback but quick as a flash, the boy replied: "Don't thi believe it, mister – I've copt four already an' they arn't arf big uns."

Edward Hinchcliffe

HERBERT SUTCLIFFE once consented to take part in a charity match between two Yorkshire village teams, and of course there was a tremendous crowd of spectators.

Batting first, Herbert thought a "six" would be fitting, and stepped down the wicket to the first ball, slipped on the "unlike test-match" turf and missed the ball completely.

The wicket-keeper avidly gathered the ball, whipped off the bails, and yelled, "Howzat!" in a voice which could be heard all over Yorkshire.

The umpire gazed at him sadly for a moment, then said, witheringly, "Not aht. Does ta think all these fowk've come to watch thee stump?"

(Miss) S.M. Thornton

ON THE FIRST DAY of the county cricket match, Yorkshire versus Glamorgan, at Harrogate, an old-age pensioner went along to pay his membership subscription. He and the secretary chatted about the good weather.

Said the secretary: "You'd have thought there'd be more people in the ground on a lovely day like this."

The pensioner replied: "I wouldn't worry; it'll fill up after lunch."

The secretary asked why that was, and the pensioner replied: "It's half day at Pateley Bridge."

Fred Trueman

CHOP YAT CRICKET TEAM, on the North York Moors, have seen good and bad times. Many years ago they dismissed Ingleby Greenhow for nil, which must be some kind of statistic for the record books. Yet a few years later, they were fielding at Chopyat, somebody hit the ball and the captain ran after it. The ball went down a rabbit hole.

The batsmen kept on running, and they ran 44 before the ball was retrieved. The wicket-keeper said: "Ye should've shouted 'lost ball' after they'd run six."

Observed the captain: "It weren't lost; ah just couldna reach it."

K.G.C.

ONE OF THE local lads was batting for his cricket team. When the ball came he would swipe at it, but in almost every case he would miss it.

One of the older members of the village who was watching said to another: "Fred isn't doing mich tiday."

"Neer," said his pal, "Ah think he'd be better mowin' t' nettles."

A.L.

TWO LOCAL FOOTBALL teams had been engaged in fierce combat for over half-an-hour when one of the visiting side was sent off limping. Immediately the home captain sent one of his men off.

"You're a real sport," remarked a supporter at half-time. "I suppose you don't like the idea of playing eleven men against ten, eh?"

"Nay, it's not like that," replied the other, "but our lads have left their money in t' dressing-room."

K.P.

NOT FAR FROM Beverley a signpost bears the legend "Hutton 1". Just before the great man's retirement an outraged local patriot added to this the words: "Not Out".

B.L.

ON AN AUGUST evening, my family and I were in Skipton. As we wandered in Newmarket Street, we saw a notice announcing a bowls tournament to be held that evening at the Devonshire Hotel.

Welcoming the opportunity to sit awhile, we entered the area at the back of the hotel and settled down to watch the tournament. We had seen some dearly contested 'ends' when my seven-year-old daughter suddenly said: "They're very good for disabled people, aren't they?"

When we enquired why she thought the players were disabled, she pointed out that the notice had said it was a 'handicap bowls tournament'.

G.G.

MY FATHER was a Wensleydale Football League referee in the league's early days, when telephones were few and far between and last-minute engagements were made by telegram.

An old gentleman called Ralph Spencely delivered the telegrams in the Reeth district and he arrived at our house in Grinton one Saturday morning with a reply-paid telegram from Teddie Webster, who was then the league secretary, asking my father if he could referee a match at Redmire that afternoon.

My father's reply was a straight "Yes," but Ralph thought that was not enough, especially as the reply allowed for up to ten paid-for words. However, as there did not seem much else to be said, they finally agreed the reply should read: "Yes, all right."

W.H.P.

FISHERMAN (TO NATIVE): "I suppose the water in the lake here is not preserved, is it?"
    Native: "Not as I knows on."
    Fisherman: "Well, then, it won't be a crime if I catch any fish?"
    Native: "No, it'll be a miracle."

F.N.

A VILLAGE JOINER was making a coffin on the death of an old inhabitant. A lad rushed into his workshop and exclaimed: "Thi brothers sent mi to tell thi a grand watter's coming doon, and he's copped six a'ready." The joiner immediately broke off work and went trout fishing. Another villager criticised his conduct. Said the joiner: "Old so-and-so kept me waiting many a long year for the job, so he can't complain if I keep him waiting an hour or two seeing there's a grand watter to be fished."

Ernest Merritt

A GARSDALE FISHERMAN, making his way home after a fruitless day's fishing, called at a friend's house.
    "Ah hevn't had a bite all t'day," he remarked.
    The lady of the house jumped to her feet exclaiming: "Eh! What! Ah'll put t' kettle on – thoo'll be fair famished."

J.A.S.

Hard at Work

HE WORKED in a West Riding textile factory. For many years he and another man had done a certain job together, but his pal had been taken ill, and so he had carried on for three months without any acknowledgment from the boss of the fact that he was doing two men's work, and certainly without any increase in salary.

At last he summed up courage to approach the master and ask for a rise.

"Yer knaw, Mista John, I'm doing two men's wark," he said, "and I hevn't had a rise for years. I'd be ashamed for anybody to knaw what yer pay me."

"Haw, don't thee worry about that, lad. Nobody knaws what I pay thi but thee an' me; an' I shan't tell nobody."

AT A DENTDALE sawmill, Joe and Ned were "throng" making a water wheel. The day wore on. Joe thought longingly of catching the early bus home to tea and slippers.

"Let's gi' owwer, Ned," he burst out at last, "Rome wasn't built in a day."

But Ned had other ideas. "Neea, it wasn't," he replied. "I wasn't foreman."

TWO LABOURERS WERE working on a very tall block of flats. Suddenly the man at the top of the ladder called to his mate at the bottom: "I say, Jim, come up 'ere a minute and listen."

His mate slowly climbed the ladder, and at last, quite out of breath, reached the top. "I can't 'ear nothing," he said after listening intently for a while.

"No," said the other. "Ain't it quiet?"

THE VILLAGE BUILDER and his son were putting a new roof on to an addition to an existing house, and being anxious to finish the slating of this, the father said he would carry on by moonlight.

The son, eager to get away, spotted a slate which his father had put on wrong side up. "Thou's gittin that wrong side up," he said to his father, "time we knocked off." "Nay," replied his father, "if it is light enough for thee to see it is wrong side up, we can carry on a bit longer yet."

T.N.

A LEEDS MAN, who had always been in the habit of being last at work, arrived as usual several minutes late the other morning.

"How is it thou's allus t' last?" asked the foreman.

"Somebody hes to be t' last," replied the man.

"That's reight enough," said the foreman.

"Well, then," replied the latecomer, "thou might as well hev somebody thou can rely on."

T.N.P.

A LONDONER watched a local blacksmith making a wrought-iron gate. The Londoner said: "It's nice to see a true craftsman at work. I work in the small instrument field, where I've got to be accurate to 1/10,000th of an inch."

The blacksmith looked at him and said: "Wheel, in that case thoo'd better stay and watch. Ah's exact."

P.N.W.

WHILE VISITING his son in London, a Dales farmer noticed four road labourers taking a breather, leaning on their shovels.

"Typical southerners," he growled, "Three doin' nowt an' one helpin' 'em."

T.M. Kearns

A MAN APPLIED for a job on a building site. The man in charge responded with the following "Irishism":

'Well! I've a man here who hasn't come, and if he doesn't come before noon I'll send him back and then tha can start."

Down on t' Farm

"On a cold morning you should warm your hands."

A FARMER'S WIFE sent a crate of eggs to a packing station, but before doing so she wrote on one of them: "I got a small return on this egg. What did you pay for it?" She added her name and address.

A year later she received her answer. It was written on the highly embellished stationery of an actor.

"My dear madam," he wrote, "while playing the part of *Hamlet* recently I received your egg for nothing."

Jack Broadley

ABOUT FIFTY YEARS AGO an old farmer in Wharfedale was noted for his indifference to his appearance. He appeared before the local magistrates for a trivial offence. The chairman, looking at the farmer with disapproval, asked: "How long do you wear your shirts?" Without hesitation came the reply: "Six inches below mi bottom."

W.S.

A WEST RIDING farmer was moodily regarding the ravaging of a flood.

"Kit," called a neighbour. "Ah've just seen all your pigs washed down the river."

"What about Robinson's pigs?" asked the farmer.

"Oh, they're gone, too."

"And Calvert's?"

"Oh, aye, they've gone."

"Ah well," said the farmer, cheering up, "maybe it isn't as bad as Ah thowt."

R.T.

THE DALES FARMER had a day of continual disappointment. "One door closes," he explained to a friend, "and another door slams shut!"

K.J.B.

A SHEPHERD entered Tan Hill Inn. Seated in the room was a young mother with a baby of tender age. Casting a glance in the direction of the child, the shepherd remarked: "Ay, lad, I wish I was as awd as thee." Then, no doubt thinking he may be mistaken about the child's sex, he addressed the mother: "Is't a tup or a gimmer?"

N.T.

AN OLD YORKSHIRE farmer was visited in his isolated farm one day by a younger acquaintance who commented on the decrepit nature of the old man's wireless set. The visitor suggested that the farmer should purchase a new one.

"Nay, lad," the farmer replied, "Ah'm ower owd for change, and Ah've nobbut just gotten used to fowk in this yun."

T.K.L.

SEVERAL YEARS AGO two men working on a farm were moving chicken arks one day when, to their horror, a rat ran from under one, and disappeared up the trouser leg of the younger man.

Petrified, he clasped his hands round the top of his leg and yelled: "Quick, do summat."

"It's alreight, lad," came the comforting reply. "Thee just 'old it theer while Ah fetch mi gun."

C.R.

"... it's made of real leather."

A DALES FARMER, well known for his excessive thrift, was on his way to Skipton market when he called at the local blacksmith's to have a foreign body removed from his eye. The blacksmith stopped work and, with a sharpened match, performed the operation. Then holding up the fly impaled on the match, he enquired:
"Will ter tack it wi' thee or call for it as tha comes back?"

T.L.M.

A DALES FARMER was asked by a neighbour how well his hens were laying. "They've stopped, every one of them," he replied.
"Can you account for it?" asked a neighbour.
"I believe I can, Tom," the farmer said. "It's like this. I've been having a small shippon built and the bricklayers have been working on piecework. I'll swear my hens were listening when them chaps were swanking about the wages they earn laying bricks."

F.L.T.

SOME BUILDERS had to go to a remote farm to do some work. They sent their youngest "lad" to hire a horse from the nearest village. After completing the deal, the owner of the horse asked:
"How long will you want it?"
"Oh," said Jack, "we shall want t' longest thoo hes. There's five on us."

E.L.T.

21

A WENSLEYDALE FARM lad bought a watch for five shillings and it was guaranteed to remain in good order for five years. At the end of the first year the lad took the watch back to the shop and announced that it wouldn't go.

"Nah then, lad, tha's 'ad an accident wi' it, hasn't ta?" queried the watchmaker.

"Aye, that's right mister. Ah did have a bit o' an accident," the lad replied. "Tha sees, six months sin' Ah were feeding t' pig and t' watch fell into t' trough."

"Six months sin'," said the watchmaker. "Thou owt t' browt it back afore now."

"Ah couldn't," said the lad, "we nobbut killed t' owd pig yesterday."

J.P.R.

A DALES SHEPHERD'S employer – a gentleman farmer – was in need of a tup and, much to the shepherd's amazement and anger, decided to trust his own judgement at the ram sale. The shepherd not only doubted his ability to select an animal most suited to the flock's requirements, but he was also vexed at being deprived of his annual visit to the sale, to which came all the shepherds from the surrounding dales.

When his master arrived back with the tup, the shepherd viewed it critically and silently from every angle. Finally having felt it in the approved style, he stepped back a few paces and asked: "Ye'll hev getten a pedigree wid it?"

"Yes, a very long pedigree," was the reply.

The shepherd threw back his head. "Ah nivver did see a toop that stood mair in need o' yan."

J.J.R.

TWO NEIGHBOURING FARMERS who hadn't seen each other for several weeks met at the cattle auction. After a few minutes the conversation turned to thrift, which shortly resulted in a heated argument.

Finally one said: "Cum ower to ar spot one neet, and Ah'll gi' thee a bit of tuition on't."

A few nights later the neighbour arrived and found his friend sitting on the only comfortable chair in the place.

"Draw that stoile up an' warm thi 'ands on t' fire."

They sat like this for several minutes then he went on: "Naw then, ah'll tell thee abaht thrift, but first of all we'll blow t' candle aht. We can talk baht leet."

F.J.

Queen's Highway

A YORKSHIREWOMAN'S CAR died on her at a junction. Repeated use of the starter failed to bring it to life again. Somewhere behind her a horn was being blown without cease. At last the lady dismounted from her vehicle and, without hurry, went in search of her tormentor. "Now, lad," she said, "thou get up yonder and re-start my car – I'll sit in thine and keep my finger on thy horn."

Katherine Farey

LANDRACE PIGS were introduced from the Continent in the early "fifties". They were considered longer and leaner than the average English pig of that date, though their import aroused some controversy. My friend and neighbour, the late Mr George Atkinson, Snilegate Head, Rievaulx, stopped his grey horse to tell me one of his many tales.

He had been rounding the bend of Newgate Foot, before the road-widening operations, when a boar pig appeared from Featherholme Farm nearby and strolled across the road. At this moment, a driver of a fast car swooped round in the opposite direction, saw the pig just in time and swerved to miss its tail by an inch. The driver pulled up and said to George: "Good job it wasn't a Landrace!" Evidently the local breed's lack of length was an advantage in modern traffic conditions.

Edward Hart

A FUNERAL PROCESSION was passing up Skipton High Street. A crowd, largely working folk, stood watching it pass. A rather well-dressed and somewhat arrogant lady visitor pushed her way through to the front and elbowed a place between two men. Turning to one, she said in a very superior voice: "Who is dead, my man?" He turned, took a good look at her, then said: "Him in t'box, missis."

E. Raistrick

AN AMERICAN TOURIST in a large limousine asked the way from an old Yorkshire villager who was trying to cut his lawn with a rusty old mower. "What di yer call that greeat thing?" said the old man. "An automobile – and what's yours called?" asked the tourist. "It's an ought ta maw grass, bud it we'ant," said the villager.

H. Hudson Rodmell

A YORKSHIREMAN and a Scotsman were involved in a motor accident while driving their respective cars on the Great North Road. The men sat on the verge rubbing their heads. The Scotsman produced a whisky flask and almost drained it before offering it to the other.

"No, thank you," came the Yorkshireman's reply, "not until the police have been."

Colonel Rupert Alec-Smith

ABOUT sixty years ago a farmer, driving his horse and trap from Pickering market, was stopped by a young policeman.

"Now what's wrang?" asked the farmer.

"Do you know you are driving without lights?"

"Aye," said the farmer. "But does thou know that Ah's as tight as a bottle, and tawd mare's as blind as a bat, sae what's good o' lights tae us?"

D.A. Wrangham

I HAD TAKEN my car in to a Wharfedale garage one day while I was on holiday there, as I had had a good deal of trouble on local hills.

When he had inspected it, I asked the garage owner how much it would be. His reply was a classic:

"Ah reckon it'll cost you a lot – and, of course, that's just an estimate."

M. Rider

A FARMER went to buy a hunter and, before completing the deal, asked to try his fancy over two or three sizeable jumps. The horse cleared the obstacles with great freedom and the transaction was sealed.

The buyer thought he would ride the horse to the railway station and, coming to a viaduct, the horse threw up its head and burst in to a canter.

Taken aback, the farmer patted the horse on the neck and pleaded: "Steady, old fellow, steady . . . *under, not over it!*"

E.R.

A FARMER and his son with tractor and trailer drove straight out of their field adjoining the A1 near Boroughbridge into the path of a Jaguar that was being driven at great speed.

The driver took evasive action by swerving into the field from which the tractor had come, and this car went down the headland and out through another gate.

The farmer turned to his son and heaved a sigh, remarking: "By gum, Johnnie – we nobbut just gat out of that field i' time."

Arthur D. Taylor

THE VILLAGE CONSTABLE had secured as a witness to an accident one of the village worthies, and the day came when the old gent had to go into the witness box.

The chairman of the bench asked him what sort of a car it was that had caused the accident.

"Nay, I doan't reightly knaw," said the old man, then with a sudden flash of inspiration, "but it wor one o' them 'pip pippin' sort."

G.H.

A NORTH YORKSHIRE farmer used to go to market each week with his horse and cart.

One day after his usual visit to the pub, and having had one over the eight, by the help of the landlord he got into the cart and set off for home. Soon he fell fast asleep.

Some youths on the way saw how things were, unyoked the horse and let it go.

Presently the farmer woke, took a puzzled look around and said: "If it's me ah've lost a hoss, an if it isn't ah've fun a cart."

A.N.

A FEW FRIENDS were discussing old folk they knew when one man said, very proudly: "My uncle is 91. He has just stopped riding his bike."

The quick reply to that was: "What's up; has 'e 'ad a puncture?"

P. Whiteley

THIS EPISODE took place on Market Street, Bradford. A stranger asked an old-time tram driver to direct him to Church Bank and received the following reply:

"Go straight on 'ear, nobbut ower thear, then rahnd t'square at t'end, then tha'll see a church just aght o' seet, turn left and yer'll be reight."

John Goldsbrough

ON A LONELY stretch of road in the Yorkshire Dales a motorist ran out of petrol and, seeing a man with a horse and cart, begged a lift.

A little further along the road the horse took fright and bolted, careering down a steep hill. "I would give £50 to be out of this mess," said the city gentleman.

To which the Yorkshireman replied: "Don't be rash wi' thee cash – tha'll be out for naught in a minute."

He was.

M. Summers

A YORKSHIRE farmer's son was staying with friends in the Forces. Members of the American forces, stationed at the same camp, organised a hay-ride to which young Sam was invited.

The excited children climbed on to two huge American army vehicles and as they settled down, a very Yorkshire voice was heard to say: "I thought we were going for a hay-ride – this is blooming oat straw!"

G.M. Blacker

ON A COACH tour of Wales, the driver stopped the coach as we skirted the base of Snowdon.

He waxed very poetical, pointing upwards: "Look you, people, is it not a wonderful sight?"

A sceptical Yorkshireman said grudgingly: "Aye, but when all's said an' done, lad, it's nowt but a lump o'muck!"

Grace C. Bingham

"Then it made a noise exactly like a shoulder strap breaking."

TRAVELLING BY CAR through the Yorkshire Dales last summer, I saw some beautiful old-fashioned flowers growing in a cottage garden. I stopped to look at them and then asked the elderly lady in the garden if I could buy a few.

Without a word she went indoors for some scissors and cut almost half of them down for me and refused my money.

When I protested, she smiled and said: "No thanks. It's the first time I remember having anything that anyone else ever wanted."

N. Whitham

A VEHICLE USED a byroad in Wensleydale one Sunday. All the available car space was filled with wild flowers, foliage and even young trees.

Uncertain of their route, they stopped by a farmer and enquired: "Should we take this road back to Leeds?"

"You might as well," replied the farmer. "It looks as if you're taking about everything else."

M.R.

WHEN I CALLED at a motorway service station for refreshment, I saw a lorry driver I knew sitting at a table.

"Hullo, Jim," I said. "What have you got there – tea or coffee?"

"Nay," replied Jim sadly. "They didn't say."

E. Ferguson

A YORKSHIREMAN, walking in the middle of a country road, was obliged to jump into the hedge bottom to avoid a car as it swept past him.

"Road hog!" he bawled.

From the car floated back on the breeze: "Hedgehog!"

R.B.

HE WAS DRIVING too fast; just scraped past the traffic lights as they changed; missed a car coming the other way by inches; dusted the side of a bus; made two pedestrians jump for their lives, and stopped at a traffic obstruction. The policeman strolled across. "Listen, cowboy," he said, producing a large white handkerchief, "next time you come this way I'll drop this and see if you can pick it up with your teeth."

R.T.P.

A TOURIST stopped his car and asked directions to the ancient church. A local youth pointed to the building, which was visible in the distance, at the end of a long drive.

"That's a lengthy drive," observed the tourist.

"Aye," said the local, "but if it was any shorter it wouldn't reach t' church."

K.J.B.

THE CAR HAD arrived at the ford and the motorist walked back a few yards to where he had seen the old man sitting and asked him if it was deep.

"Only a few inches," was the reply.

Three feet from the side, the bonnet was almost submerged.

"Well," said the old man, "that's proper funny, that is. That theer watter onny goes 'alfway oop our ducks."

J.T.

AN OLD LADY asked a constable if he could see her over the road. He replied: "Just a moment; I'll go across and have a look."

Magazine of North Yorkshire Police

In Transit

"There, but for the grace of God, go we."

IN THE DAYS when a coach trip was regarded with the same feelings we apply to Concorde, the small hamlet of Timble – standing desolate on the Blubberhouse moors – organised a coach trip to London. Two friends joined the party, but on arrival in the metropolis one of them became separated from his friend, and was left, quite bewildered, on a crowded pavement.

Finally, plucking up courage, he sought the help of a policeman. "Hi!" said this bewildered Yorkshireman. "'As tha seen Andrew Dickinson?" "I'm afraid I don't know Andrew Dickinson," came the reply.

"Tha doesn't knaw Andrew Dickinson o' Timble?" repeated the other, incredulously.

"Timble, where's that?" asked the amused bobby. "Tha's nivver heard o' Timble awther!" exclaimed the proud countryman with wonderment. Then: "I'll tell thee what, lad, tha'll live i' Lunnen till tha knaws nowt!"

D.N.

A YORKSHIREMAN going from York to Liverpool arrived at York station booking office. He asked for a single ticket to Liverpool.

The booking clerk threw the man the ticket, saying: "Change at Leeds." The Yorkshireman quickly replied: "Ah'll ev it noo, if yer dean't mind!" And he held his hand out for the change.

S.M.

A DALES village was two miles from the railway station, with only one bus a day.

A farmer asked his neighbour, who was going that way with a pony and trap, if he could ask if a parcel was waiting for him in the post office.

"Of course I will," he said, and in the evening, when he returned, he just yelled out as he passed: "Yes, it's there alreight."

C.E.

A SWALEDALE man bought a very second-hand car and proudly took a sceptical friend for a ride to display its good points. They laboured up hills and slid down dales. Then something passed them.

"What was that whizzed by?" asked the proud car owner.

"Nay, Ah don't rightly know," said his pal, "but I think it was a traction engine."

M.R.

I WAS WAITING to see a friend on a bus at Salterhebble, Halifax. The next bus arriving was one going to Norland. The first people in the queue were obviously a farmer and his wife. The conductor called out: "One only, please."

After a few protests from us all, the farmer jumped on to the bus and, turning to his wife and holding out his hand, said: "Gie us key, lass; I'll be get'n kettle on 'til thee gets 'oame."

She had about four miles to walk!

D.O.

OLD JOHN, HURRYING towards the railway station, was overtaken by a younger neighbour.

"Hey, Fred," he called, "will ta book me a return ticket?"

"Where to?" asked Fred.

"Back 'ere, yer fooil," replied John.

T.C.

YEARS AGO, I was commuting to York. The bus from Leeds to Scarborough was often more comfortable than the local bus from York to Rillington, but the bus inspectors were keen to get the schoolchildren on to the Rillington bus. The inspector approached a group of us and asked one girl:

"Where you going to?"

"Seamer," she replied.

As the inspector continued down the queue, someone nudged her and said: "You ain't off ti Seamer." She replied: "Ah is. Ah's off to see ma mother."

M.B.

I DRIVE A MINIBUS at an outdoor education centre. One day we took the children to Great Ayton. They were given a conducted tour of the village and learned all about Captain Cook and his adventures.

Later that evening, the children were writing up their daily diaries. One child wrote: "We walked up to Captain Cook's Monument, visited the Captain Cook museum and the house where he lived. Mr. Cook drove us home."

K.G. Cook

Overheard on t' Bus

HEARD ON A Pudsey bus:
 "Ee, luv, Ah feels reight 'olla inside."
 "Aye ... that's the worst of eating nowt on an empty stomach."

C.W.

HEARD ON A bus tour through Wensleydale:
 "That's the oldest inn there."
 "The oldest in where?"
 "The oldest in here."
 "What – here or there?"
 "Gosh, let's get out and have a drink."

H.W.

OVERHEARD ON A bus between Skipton and Leyburn: "Nah then, 'ow do you like livin i' Leyburn?"
 "It's alreight, but it's quiet after 'Ubberholme."

F.N.

DO YOU KNOW Sir Malcolm Sargent?" said a passenger on a Dales bus.
 "Who?"
 "Malcolm Sargent, the conductor."
 "No, who's he for, *t'Ribble or t'United?*"

B.N.

A WOMAN was returning from a shopping expedition in Bradford. The bus approached the stop where she wanted to alight but she was rather slow in getting up from her seat.
 Up piped the voice of the perky conductor: "If you had more leaven in your lump, madam, you'd rise better."
 "Young man," came the instant reply, "if you were better bred, you wouldn't have made that remark."

J.W.

"You keep saying: 'Don't cross your bridges until we come to them'. Well . . . we've come to them."

Market Days

"The man at the shop said it was a sheep dog."

A FARMER AND his daughter were loading up after market day in Skipton.

"Are them piglets in?" said he.

"All secure," said she.

"Did you collect them tools?" said he.

"Under t'seat," said she.

"We've got t'bran and t'meal?" said he.

"Aye, I think that's t'lot," said she.

"Then, off we go," said he, and they jogged quietly along the road towards Grassington. Still the farmer seemed uneasy and kept looking round in to the cart.

"What's up?" said she.

"Nay, I feel uneasy somehow," said he, "as if we'd forgotten summat."

When they arrived home, he jumped down from the cart, and as he began to unload, he slapped his thigh and exclaimed: "Well, I'm blessed. I know now what were bothering me. We've left yer mother i' Skipton."

B.K.M.

A YORKSHIRE FARMER was taking great interest in a pen of goats at the local market. He saw five kids and an adult. The farmer had just ascertained that the five kids were all billies when the auctioneer walked by.

"It's a pity all them kids are billies," remarked the farmer, "but I must say yon goat's done well to rear 'em."

"It's done marvellously," said the auctioneer, "seeing it's a billy as well."

T.P.

WHEN I WAS a boy, the old gentleman across the street died. A neighbour some few doors away called to extend sympathy to the bereaved and to offer any help, as may be expected at times like these. The offer was promptly taken up by the deceased's daughter, who was up to her elbows catering for the anticipated influx of relations expected to attend the funeral.

"I wonder if you would call in the market and buy me a wreath, Gertie. You can see how throng I am." "Certainly, what sort of price were you thinking of?" "Oh, I don't know... twelve and six, fifteen bob, I'll leave it with you."

It was a delicate commission, indeed, thought our good Samaritan as she proceeded towards the swing doors of Kirkgate Market. "Now then, Missus, can't you mek your mind up?" It was the stallholder speaking, aware that the lady in question had already passed his colourful display four times. "Any price yer like, luv, three an' a tanner to three quid, and every bloom kissed by this mornin's dew."

He took a sip from his mug of steaming tea and, prompted by the anticipation of a sale, he continued: "Is it for someone yer loved?" "Not at all. It's for somebody that's baking!"

Horsfordian

IT WAS market day in a Yorkshire town. Two farmers, having carried out a business deal, went into the village inn to seal the transaction with a drink. Suddenly two men burst in and announced: "This is a hold-up."

Quick as lightning, one of the farmers stuck something into his friend's pocket, saying: "Here, Fred, take this."

"What is it?" whispered Fred.

"The £10 I owe you," he replied.

Alan Gostick

"THIS," said a salesman in a West Riding market, "is a universal solvent. It will dissolve anything."

"By gow, it sounds all reet," said a listener. "But I wonder what yon chap keeps it in."

E.M.T.

THE SECOND-HAND market was held in a narrow street which was always referred to as 'The Alley', so when a friend saw Bill sporting a pair of 'new' leggings, he asked: "Where did you get the gaiters from, Bill?"

"Oh I got 'em down t' Alley," said Bill.

"Then they'll be Alligators," said his friend.

Now Bill hadn't been in the front row when brains were given out, and it wasn't until he was getting into bed that night that the penny dropped. Alley gaiters, o' course – Alligators! Bill burst out laughing. "Oh! I must tell old Bert that one."

So he dressed, and he was still laughing when he reached his pal's home a couple of streets away. It was getting on towards midnight when he knocked on Bert's door. After a few minutes, Bert popped his head out of the bedroom window and called sleepily: "What's ta want, Bill?"

"This'll kill yer," said Bill. "See these new leggins I got i' market yesterday?"

"Aye," said Bert.

"Well, doesn't ta see – they're Crocodiles," said Bill. "Tha warn't see it at furst, but tha'll laugh thi sides sooer i' t' morning."

J.C.

A Class of their Own

IT WAS a hot summer day. The children were restless. Suddenly there was a commotion at the back of the class, and a hand shot up.
"Miss, Janice has got an ice-cream in her pocket!"
Miss (almost dumbfounded): "Why Janice?"
Janice: "Please, Miss, I'm saving it for playtime!"

A DALES CLASS was being told about Jacob and the ladder he dreamed about, when he pictured angels ascending and descending.
"Please, Miss," said a small boy, "why did yon angels have to climb when they've getten wings?"
"Don't be so daft," said a little girl, "they must have bin in t' moult."

B.N.F.

HERE IS a story from my Nidderdale classroom:
' "What tree grows from a conker?" asked Ruth, one morning.
"Horse chestnut," I replied, adding: "Funny, isn't it? I wonder why we call them conkers."
A sort of ruminating silence followed, and then a lad volunteered, thoughtfully: "Well, it could be named after somebody. There was a man called William the Conker, you know."

M.L.

A TEACHER friend of mine seemed to take great delight in recounting this anecdote from her training days.
A rather "big-headed" fellow student was asked to take some children on a nature walk. Pausing by a wall, and looking up at a tree growing over it, she said: "Now, children, just look at this lovely copper beech tree."
As the children duly stood and looked, a man's voice said: "Nay, Miss, but it's noan a copper beech – it's a purple ploom!"

B.K.G.

ONE WET PLAYTIME at school, Michael fell over in the playground. He came in to school wet through and covered in mud. The teacher went to his assistance. "Michael – however did you manage to make such a mess of yourself?" she asked. Michael replied: "'Twas easy, Miss."

M.B.

A DALES SCHOOLTEACHER had punished Tommy so often for talking during school, and the punishment had been so apparently without effect, that as a last resort she decided to notify Tommy's father of his son's fault. So following the deportment mark on his next report, there were these words: "Tommy talks a great deal."

In due time the report was returned with his father's signature, and under it was written:

"You ought to hear his mother."

P.R.S.

MY FATHER was the first headmaster of the newly opened council school in Garforth. Having occasion, one day, to go through into the infants' school, he met a very small boy, younger brother of a pupil in the 'big' school.

Looking down at him from his height of six feet, my father said sternly: "I hear you've been a naughty boy!"

Instead of the expected head hung in shame, he got an indignant look as the small boy blazed up at him: "Who telled thee? Our Dick?"

K.B.

A SCHOOL INSPECTOR, visiting one of the schools in Wensleydale, asked the teacher of the class to introduce him to the brightest boy in the class with a view to testing him on his mental arithmetic.

So the inspector asked the boy: "If you had 25p in your right-hand trouser pocket, 50p in your left one, and 60p in your hip pocket, what would be the amount of money you had?"

Like lightning the boy replied: "Nowt, Sir, as they wouldn't be my trousers."

K.P.

THE SCHOOLCHILDREN had been singing their evening hymn before school closed. After they had chanted the "Amen", and the teacher was preparing to dismiss the class, a thoughtful-looking child suddenly asked, "Why do we always say 'Amen' and not 'Awomen'?"

Before the teacher could reply, the little girl next to her volunteered an explanation: "That's because they're 'ims," she said, "and not 'ers."

R.A.

HEARD IN A DALES school:
  Teacher: "'I come to bury Caesar, not to praise him.' Who said that?"
  Boy: "Please, Sir, the undertaker."

V.W.

"He said his first words today – metaphysical philosophy!"

SMALL BILL, AT Cowgill School, Dent, could not – and would not – count. His teacher, noticing his pride in his new blazer with shining gilt buttons, thought, "Here is the way."

"One, two, three, four, five, six," she counted, as she pretended to pull off his precious buttons, one by one, into her hand. "Now, Bill," she asked, "how many buttons have I?"

"A gert han'ful," replied Bill.

P.R.S.

A TEACHER AT a West Riding school was pointing out that a surname often indicated the trade of the ancestors of those who bore the name. He gave, as examples, Smith, Taylor, Baker and others. Then he questioned one of the boys.

"What were your ancestors, Webb?"
"Spiders, Sir."

L.D.

A LITTLE BOY had to apologise in a letter for forgetting his aunt's birthday. So he wrote: "I'm sorry I forgot your birthday. I have no excuse and it will serve me right if you forget mine next Friday."

A.F.

A WEST RIDING schoolmaster, wanting to impress on his pupils the need of thinking before speaking, told them to count to 50 before saying anything important, and 100 if it was very important.

A few days later he was speaking with his back to the fire when he noticed several lips moving rapidly. Suddenly the whole class shouted: "Ninety-nine, a hundred; your coat's on fire, sir."

C.A.M.

YOUNG JOHNNY WAS very reluctant to go to school. To delay the process, he went the long way round through the fields, and ignoring the footpath, he scrambled through the hedges, getting very tattered in the process. On arriving at school he found all the others had gone in, and looking through the window he saw the teacher just writing. Quietly opening the door, he tiptoed to his place.

Unfortunately, the teacher glanced up and looking at Johnny and then at the clock, he said: "Johnny, I see you're behind."

Turning round, Johnny replied defiantly: "Tha wudn't if Ah'd hed another safety pin."

T.Q.

AFTER GIVING a lesson on building to a class in a Yorkshire school, the teacher, seeing Johnny hadn't been paying much attention, asked him if he could give three different examples of types of windows usually found in houses. After a quick thought, Johnny replied: "Yes, sir. Oppun, shut, and brokkun."

R.S.L.

AT A DALES school at the end of the year a teacher set his class of sixteen-year-olds a test. Apparently it was a stiff test – too stiff for one pupil who looked at the paper for half an hour, then shrugged his shoulders and wrote across it: "God knows, I don't. Merry Christmas." He then walked out.

When the results were up on the notice-board at the beginning of the new term opposite his name was written: "God passed, you didn't. Happy New Year."

J.F.T.

The Age of Chivalry

"There now – isn't that more manly?"

A WOMAN IN a station refreshment room was struggling with a cup of hot coffee as her train came in. She endeavoured to gulp it quickly.

A dalesman sitting at the next table noticed her plight. He leaned across to her and said: "Here, mum, you tak' my cup o' coffee. Ah've already saucered and blowed it."

41

A LAD HAD taken his lass to the local cinema, but the lass arrived home in tears.

"Wot's up?" asked her mother.

"He only took me in t' tanners," she complained.

"Well, 'ere's sixpence: tek it straight to 'is 'ouse and give 'im it," said the mother indignantly. "He mebbe needs it more than we do."

The lass arrived at the house, knocked on the door, and her cinema escort answered the knock.

"I've browt your tanner back," she said. "Mother says you may need it more nor we do."

"Nay," said he, "you needn't have bothered to-neet. It'd 'ave done in t' morning."

A SOLDIER FROM north of the Border made the acquaintance of a girl in a Yorkshire town where he was stationed. He courted her for some time and eventually plucked up enough courage to propose to her. But when the moment came it seemed a little difficult.

"I was here on Monday night, wasn't I, Mary?" he began.

"Of course."

"And I was here again on Tuesday night."

"That's so."

"And I was back again on Wednesday night."

"You were, Ian."

"Now this is Friday and I am here again. Oh, Mary, d'ye no smell a rat?"

A.N.F.

AN IRISHMAN WENT to a social. He danced all the jigs and reels with the same girl. Finally he asked if he might escort her home. She agreed, saying that her home was seven miles away.

After walking about one and a half miles, he asked for a kiss. There the trouble began. She was six feet three inches tall and he but three feet six inches.

However, he saw a row of milk churns and, climbing on to one, he gave her a stunner. They proceeded a further three miles, and he asked to be favoured by another. "Oh no," said she, "one night, one kiss."

"If that's the case," said he, "I can drop this churn."

P.M.B.

Wedded Bliss

"It's her fifth wedding."

ONE DAY A clergyman visited a house and found a man and his wife having what is known in some parts as a "reight fratch".

"Come, come," said the minister, "this won't do."

He then pointed out the dog and cat sleeping peacefully by the hearth and said: "Just look at these two, how peaceful they are."

"Aye," said the husband, "but thee tie them together and then see what 'appens."

T.R.

A MAN DASHED into a Dales police station at midnight. "My wife," he gasped. "Will you find my wife. She's been missing since eight this evening. I must find her!"

"Particulars?" asked the sergeant. "Height?"

"I – I don't know."

"Do you know how she was dressed?"

"No, but she took the dog with her."

"What kind of a dog?"

"Brindle, bull terrier, weight 53 pounds, four dark blotches on his body shading from grey to white, three white legs, and right front leg brindled all but the toes. A small nick in his left ear."

"That'll do," gasped the sergeant.

Fred Smithson

THERE WAS a youngish farmer's lad who was courting a lass in upper Airedale. He couldn't afford to get married on his wages, so he found a job on the railway at Leeds, with the promise of a cottage near the shunting lines.

They were married and went to live in the cottage. It was only a matter of days before the young wife said she couldn't stand the noise of shunting, day and night.

"Never mind, lass," said the husband. "Thee get back to thi mother and stay theer till tha gets used to it."

E. Vickerman

A MAN WANTED a divorce from his wife because she kept goats. The solicitor said there were no grounds for divorce because she kept goats.

"Oh, but she keeps them in t' bedroom and they smell."

"Couldn't you open the window?" the solicitor said.

"What," said the applicant, "and let all my pigeons out. No fear."

K.R.

JONT WENT a-courting the Dent schoolmistress. Each evening as she sat knitting, Jont pulled out her needles, letting her stitches drop. Always without reproach but with seemingly unending patience, Mary picked up the stitches and knitted it up again. This continued week after week. Jont boasted to his pals that he'd "getten t'best-tempered woman i' t' world".

The wedding day dawned. As they walked home over the bridge after the ceremony, Mary turned to Jont, her eyes blazing – but not with love – and snarled: "Now Ah'll ravel thee."

THE PITHY REMARK of a West Riding man: "Aye, man's a lump of clay. Woman taks him an' maks him into a mug."

T.N.

THE PROS AND CONS of marriage were being discussed with a local bride-to-be. She said: "Marriage is like my mother's clipped mats – you've got ti stick at it till it's finished."

HE STOOD AT the fountain-pen counter of a Bradford store making a careful choice. "You see," he explained to the assistant, "I'm buying a present for my wife."
　"A surprise, perhaps?" replied the assistant.
　"I'll say so," was the answer. "She's expecting a new car."

T.N.

SOON AFTER THE arrival of his first baby, the Dales farmer's wife went upstairs one evening and found him standing by the cot gazing earnestly in to it.
　She was very touched by the sight, and tears filled her eyes. Her arm stole softly round him. He started slightly at the touch, and she asked him what he was thinking.
　"Nay, lass," he said sadly. "It beats me how they can reckon to ask five punds for a cot like that."

H.T.

At the Coast

A YOUNG Yorkshire lady who was planning to go on holiday to Scarborough with her girl friend was bitterly disappointed when, a week or so before the date of departure, her friend cried off. However, her mother suggested that she put an advertisement in the local paper reading: "Attractive young lady seeks companion for holiday in Scarborough." This she did, under a box number.

Some days later, she was reading through some replies to the advertisement when she burst out laughing. "What's the matter?" asked her mother. "Well," replied the girl, "there's one here from Dad."

David Jenkinson

"Has anyone handed in a boat?"

A VISITOR to Scarborough got in to conversation with one of the old fishermen on the West Pier and they were talking generally about Scarborough as a fishing community. The fisherman went on to say that his family line had been traced back to the year 1200 and that they had always been associated with Scarborough's fishing industry.

The visitor then jokingly remarked: "I suppose if you go back far enough, you will find that one of your ancestors sailed with Noah in the Ark." To which the fisherman replied: "I don't think so; you see, we've always had our own boat."

Len Dobson

BEFORE THE ADVENT of motor-coach travel there were people in Cawood who had never been further than walking distance from the village. Their main recreational activity was standing at the edge of the River Ouse, gazing at the opposite bank and discussing the topics of the day.

Three of these little-travelled countrymen were persuaded to join a coach party from a local inn to Scarborough. On arrival they walked down to the south side and stood, thumbs in belts, gazing silently out to sea.

Eventually one of the trio said in wonderment, "By gor, lads, she's a hell of a width!"

R.P.T.

OVERHEARD at a small North Yorkshire fishing village:
"Wat's ta bin doin' this afternoon, George?"
"Oh, just lookin' fer a bit o' jet on t' beach."
"Wat's ta get fer it now?"
"Six shillings a pund."
"Oh, tha doesn't want ta sell it yet. They'll be giving a good price fer it soon. They're flying aeryplanes on it now, tha knaws."

K.T.

WHEN the German Navy had bombarded Scarborough in 1914, the German press claimed a victorious levelling of "a fortified town" (one paper described Scarborough as "the most important harbour on the east coast of England between the Humber and the Thames, protected by a mole and batteries"!).

A townsman had the last facetious word. He put up a notice on his shell-damaged home: "Please don't touch the fortifications – Fragile."

Ian Dewhirst

AN AMERICAN approached a fisherman on the quayside at Whitby and, pointing up to the Westcliff hotels, asked: "What are those places?" When told they were some of the best hotels, he laughed and said: "We are building bigger fish and chip shops in the States."

Next day the American came to the same fisherman and, pointing to the two lighthouses on the piers, asked what they were. The answer came back quickly: "They're salt and pepper pots for thy fish and chip shops."

Eric Turner

TOMMY AND HIS MOTHER were walking along the sea front.
"What's that over there, Mummy?" he asked.
"That's a lighthouse," explained his mother.
"What's it for?"
"To keep the ships from getting on the rocks."
There was a short pause then Tommy said: "We ought to get one for Daddy."

T.S.

"Can't you get them to change the holiday rota?"

Church and Chapel

> "You can't frighten them with Hell Fire. They're used to central heating..."

A BISHOP was on holiday in the Dales country. He was in mufti when he fell in to step and in to conversation with a local man. As they walked along, they talked of this and that. At one point, the bishop asked the other what his occupation was. "Why, Ah's a shepherd," he replied, and added: "What might you be?"

"I suppose you could say I was also a shepherd," said the bishop with a smile. "Why, noo, mister," said the countryman enthusiastically, "and what sik a tuppin' time hasta had?"

Alan Donaldson

THE OCCASION was the performance of the annual chapel *Messiah*, and platform space was very limited. The late John Paley, that lovable giant of a man, revelled in the aria "The trumpet shall sound" and left his hearers in no doubt that "The dead shall be raised incorruptible".

At rehearsal, limbering up, so to say, for his great moment, John raised his long ceremonial trumpet to his lips, and thereupon realised that when extended to playing position, the bell of his instrument would barely miss the ear of the principal cellist. The fortissimo climax would surely blow the said cellist right out of the chapel on to the Yorkshire moors.

Choosing an appropriate moment, John leaned forward, tapped the endangered player on the shoulder and remarked: "Ah say, George, if ah wer thee, ah'd SHIFT!"

Arthur Percival

A CHILD became separated from her parents on a busy afternoon in York Minster. A message was put out over the tannoy: "Would the parents of....." A little lad standing in the nave turned to his parents and asked: "Was that Jesus speaking?"

Rev. Bernard Croft

AN OLD-TIME preacher had walked several miles to preach at a small chapel in the country. His congregation consisted of one dear old lady. Should he take the service or have a few words of prayer and return home?

The preacher decided it was his duty to preach. He went through the full service. When the last hymn was announced, the dear old lady began to look uncomfortable, for it was that beginning: "Come, O thou traveller unknown", and including the words: "With thee all night I mean to stay and wrestle till the break of day".

"But tha' weent," shot back the old lady as she made for the door, "'cos I'm off 'ome."

Samuel Cheesbrough

IN KANO, on the edge of the Sahara, one of the two bank managers during the 1939-45 war was from the East Riding. Each evening he arrived in the small club shortly before 6pm to listen to the news on the overseas service of the B.B.C. Each evening he listened without comment to an unending story of disaster.

Then came the night on which we heard: "Last night there was a Baedeker raid on York; details of damage have not yet been released."

To the astonishment of all present, except for fellow Yorkshiremen like myself, the pipe was removed, the glass set down. "By gum," he said, "if they've got t'minster there'll be hell to pay."

Stanhope White

A SPINSTER, who had been listening with delight to the Salvation Army Band outside Morley Town Hall, put a pound note in the hat that was taken round. The bandmaster thanked her profusely and said: "Hallelujah, that's reight good on yer missus. Yer can choose onny hymn yer want. What'll it be?"

"I'll hev 'im what plays big drum," was the unexpected reply.

Ken Lemmon

TWO METHODIST PREACHERS were being entertained to dinner by a local farmer. The farmer's wife had done them proud with two of their own reared chickens. During the dinner the farmer received an emergency call to his stock, and when he returned the visitors had eaten so heartily they had cleared the lot and he had to make do with corned beef.

He felt a bit disgruntled but after the meal he took them round his poultry enterprise. The two men praised the excellency of his stock, especially his male bird. "Aye," said the farmer, thinking of his corned beef dinner, "he ought to feel proud of hissen; he had two sons in t'ministry."

W. Stockdale

IN A COMPARATIVELY small Yorkshire town, a newly appointed minister was preaching for the first time at a small chapel. When he had shaken hands with the people, a little boy went boldly up to him and said that his mother had told him that he was to bring the minister home to dinner. Mother could not come to the service herself as she was busy getting the dinner ready.

The minister, a slightly pompous type, found it very difficult to speak to children. As they walked along, he failed to make any conversation, so the little boy rose to the occasion.

"I know what we're going to have for dinner, sir."

"Well, what will it be my boy?" was the reply. "Jam roly-poly," said the lad. "And how do you know that, my boy?" "Well, Mother only had one stocking on this morning."

Hubert Dumville

AN OLD-TIME VERGER at Kettlewell wor fettling up one morning when t'bishop walked in and chatted for a bit; just before he left, he said, in his best bishop-like style: "Do you get many here for early morning devotion?" "Just neah and agean," replied the verger. "I copped two on 'em at it last Tuesday morning, but I soon 'ad 'em aht."

Arnold Pickles

ON A BLEAK DAY 150 years ago, a funeral procession passed through snow to a church six miles away, reaching the building after darkness had fallen. The church door was locked. The bearers went to the vicarage to report their arrival, but the vicar flatly refused to turn out in the darkness and snow to take the service.

The men pleaded with the vicar to let them have the key so that they could leave the coffin in the church overnight. They reported to the vicar: "The coffin is safely in the church now; you can do what you like with it, we're off home!" In no time the vicar was out with his storm lantern and by its flickering rays, conducted the much-delayed funeral.

Archdeacon Arthur Sephton

A LEEDS PARSON preached on "Faith" and "Fact", beginning: "Ye're all here in t'church sitting i' front o' me, and that's a fact. That I am addressing you from t'pulpit is a fact, too, but only Faith makes me believe you are actually listening."

Simon Lindley

"How do you mean, you feel wicked?"

NOT A GREAT LOVER of clergy get-togethers, I like to tell the story of the Yorkshire farmer churchwarden who saw a dozen or more parish priests gathered at the vicarage for a chapter meeting. This worthy confided in his vicar afterwards that in his opinion clery were like muck. "Not much good in a heap, but they do a power of good when spread!"

Bernard Croft

TWO CHURCHWARDENS were touring the outlying farms of the parish. They met two Dales farmers who were leaning on a gate. One of the farmers asked a warden: "What's t'after?" "We're collecting for the church."

"Ah've nowt fer thee," came the prompt reply.

As they turned to go, the farmer called after them: "What's it for, anyhow?"

"A going-away present for the vicar," they answered.

"Come 'ere," says the farmer, "Ah'll give thee summat."

Rev. William Ruck

TWO OLD DALESMEN received personal invitation cards from their vicar to attend a special gathering, with the letters R.S.V.P. at the bottom. They were puzzled by the meaning of the letters but eventually one of them arrived at the following solution:

"Don't you know what that means, Joe? Sitha, that's French for 'Refreshments Supplied by the Vicar of the Parish'."

T.N.P.

THE FARMER was entertaining the visiting local preacher and noticed that he ate scarcely anything at teatime. "I never eat much when I'm going to preach. I find I do better if I take only a small meal," he explained.

Neither the farmer nor his wife were able to accompany the gentleman to the service, and so twelve-year-old John was sent to represent the household. On his return his father asked: "Well, what kind of a sermon did you have, John?"

"Why, t'were all right," he said.

"What d'yer mean, all reight?" asked his father.

"Well, it wor noan so bad, but he mud as weel a' etten!"

A PARROT, WHICH unfortunately was given to using bad language, was owned by two ladies, and the only way to stop the bird talking was to cover its cage with a cloth. This they made a point of doing every Sunday for the whole of the day.

One Monday morning just after the cover had been removed, a knock was heard at the door, and through the window the ladies saw it was the minister from the place where they worshipped. Their first thought was to cover up the bird in the cage, and as the reverend gentleman came into the room where the bird was, a voice from under the cloth was heard to say: "That's been a b— short week!"

T.L.

Hired Hands

ONE SUMMER, when they wor getting t'hay in at a Conistone farm, they hed an Irishman working for them. They wor putting a stack up in the field. They'd just abaht got it as high as they wanted, and when it was almost dark they tewk t'ladders away for a bit of fun, leaving t'Irishman and a rather simple chap on t'top o' t'stack.

They walked all round and round t'top of t'stack, and t'Irishman got all flustered. "How are we going to get off?" "Ow?" replied the other. "Just shut your eyes and walk abaht."

YORKSHIRE FARMER, KNOCKING hard on bedroom door of hired hand, very early in the morning: "Cum on, lad, it's time tha wer' up."
  Voice from within (very muffled): "What time is it?"
  "Half past fower."
  "Aw. Is it raining?"
  "No, it isn't."
  "Is it snawing?"
  "Naw."
  "Is it foggy?"
  "Naw, it isn't," said the farmer getting very rattled.
  "Aw, well, is it Sunday?"
  "Naw, is isn't Sunday," retorted the farmer after an abrupt silence.
  "Weel then, Ah'm badly," said the voice rather triumphantly.

Michael Thomas

A FARMER kept a number of hired men, and there were some masons working on the farm as well. The farmer summoned his men to dinner by blowing a whistle. A mad rush developed. One day a man stumbled and fell on his hands. He got up none the worse, but didn't go on for his dinner. A mason asked him why he did not continue his journey.
  "Nay, it's no use goin' now," said the man. "There'll be nowt left!"

A.S.

A NORTH RIDING farmer was requiring help on his farm and advertised in the local Press for a farm lad to live in. Two days later he was interviewing the only applicant. While discussing terms, the lad said: "I might as well tell thee, I have two bad faults. One is I'm a bad getter-up and the other is I'm not much good when I do get up."
  The farmer replied: "Thou'll be all reet by the time I get thi feet on t'cold floor at half past fower for a few mornings."
  On the first morning at work, the farmer and the lad set off to trim the hedges in the far field. After the lad had made a few unorthodox strokes with the slasher, the farmer, fearing some injury, said: "Thou go back to t'farm and t'missus 'll find thee a job around t'house. Oh, and as thou passes turnip field tak a turnip home fo' dinner."
  The lad asked: "How big a turnip should I tak?"
  The farmer, by this time exasperated, said: "Tak yan as big as thee 'eead."
  About two hours later, the postman was passing. On seeing the farmer, he stopped with a very puzzled expression on his face and said: "What's that lad of thine doing? He's got half thi field of turnips up and he's trying his hat on 'em all."

B.C.

ABE, A SIMPLE-MINDED youth who did odd jobs for the local blacksmith in a small Yorkshire town, was given an old watch by his employer. One day Abe arrived at the smithy and announced sadly: "T' watch 'as stopped, Mr. Cawthra."

"Then we'd better 'ave a look at it, lad," said the blacksmith, removing the back of the watch.

Inside was a small dead fly.

Abe's eyes widened.

"Ee, noa wonder it's stopped," he said slowly, "t' driver's deead."

J.K.

"Are you the 'Local Authority'?"

Doctor in the House

A MAN WAS sitting in the comfortably crowded waiting room of a Dales doctor's surgery when a newcomer entered, looked around carefully and said: "Isn't Mrs. Brown here?"

One of the row of women knitters looked up from her knitting and explained: "No, she's poorly today."

A DOCTOR FRIEND found that a young Dales couple were unduly anxious about their ailing baby. The doctor stayed with them throughout the night until the little one improved.

"You'll find he'll be all right when he's had a sleep," said the doctor, and he hurried home to snatch a little rest.

He was sleeping soundly when a shower of pebbles at the window awakened him abruptly. He hurried to look out.

"It's all right, doctor," beamed the young father from the garden. "I've just run dahn to tell thee t'baby's sleepin' reight peaceful!"

A DALES PLUMBER was roused at night by the local doctor, who reported that there was a blockage in his toilet. The plumber protested about the lateness of the hour, but the doctor was adamant that something should be done about it immediately.

The plumber arrived at the doctor's house, and with the doctor looked at the blocked toilet. Then the plumber remarked: "I'll tell thee what: I'll drop an aspro down yon toilet, and if it's not better in t'morning, give me another ring!"

T.K. Smith

AN OLD YORKSHIREMAN wandered slowly home from a visit to the doctor's with the verdict of his consultation sitting heavily on his mind. On reaching home he found his wife working busily upstairs. Going to the foot of the stairs he cried out: "I say, lass, I'm bahn to 'ev t'appendicitis."

Quickly the retort came from above:

"Tha's heving nowt till ah've 'ed mi noo 'at."

C.F.

MY UNCLE, in his Sheffield youth, had been given an anaesthetic by his dentist, and was advised to take it easy for the rest of the day. However, he played football and then went out for the evening, returning after the rest of the family had gone to bed.

He had just made it through the front door before collapsing unconscious in the hall. His mother heard the door open and went to the top of the stairs.

On seeing her beloved youngest prostrate – and having risen too quickly – she fainted, sliding downstairs as she fell. My aunt heard the thud and she, too, dashed up to see what was going on.

The shock of finding the "bodies" of her mother and brother proved too much for her, and she swooned on the landing.

The rest of the family emerged to find grandad ranting in his nightshirt, shrieking: "They're going down like bloody ninepins!"

J.S.

Down at t'Local

THE CITY MAN came out of the village "local" with a pal to walk to their lodgings. There was a weird scream out of the night and the city man jumped.
"What was that?" he gasped.
"An owl," said his pal.
"Yes, I know. But what was 'owling?"

J.C.

IT WAS the practice of an East Riding farmer to visit the village local for a drink each alternate Sunday evening, and then after a chat with one or two friends, to walk the two miles home.

On one occasion he stayed a little later than usual, drank a little more than usual, and set off a little more unsteady than usual. It was a very dark night and raining slightly when, about halfway to his home, he collided with a ram which had strayed on to the road.

Not knowing what he was up against, and being slightly drunk, he shot out his hand and, touching the ram's horns, took a firm hold. There was a short struggle, the ram broke free, and after slithering about on the loose gravel, made off on a grass verge.

The farmer went home and not a word about the incident was said until he visited the local again, and the barmaid asked him how he arrived home the previous time. "All right, lass," he said, "but if I meet that bloke on his bicycle again, I shall not let go of the handlebars as easily as I did last time."

L.M.

A MOTORIST who stopped for a drink at a wayside pub in Yorkshire was surprised to see that a dog of a native wore brown boots. "Brown boots for a dog!" he exploded. "But why?" pressed the visitor.

The native offered to answer the question if the visitor would buy him a pint, and after a bit of quibbling the visitor agreed to do so. "He's wearing brown boots," the native at last explained, "because I've had to take his black 'uns to be mended."

B.A.

AN OLD MAN, living alone in his small cottage, was very fond of his daily drink at the local inn. After one such visit, he slept rather too late next morning.

His neighbour, at midday, asked him about his health.

"I've a shocking head," said the toper. "If I'd known I felt so bad, I wouldn't have woken up so early!"

I.B.

TWO AGING DALESMEN met in the city and, not having seen each other for a long time, celebrated with a drink at the local pub. They talked about old times and the folk they both once knew. Soon they were well primed with ale and parted with the following conversation:

"Well, it's bin grand seein' thi agean, Bob, but Ah've bin goin' to ask thi afore, does ta ivver 'ear owt o' Joe Murgatroyd?"

"Joe Murgatroyd? What's his name?"

"Nay, Ah 'ad it on t' tip o' mi tongue a minute sin'."

A.J.N.

TWO YORKSHIREMEN HAD taken rather too much to drink and as they stumbled along a country road, they had a heated argument about what they saw in the heavens.

One asserted it was the sun, while the other was equally certain that it was the moon.

Seeing another man approaching, they appealed to him. One of them said: "Ah say, mister, isn't that t'sun?"

The other one chimed in: "Nay, it's t'mooin, isn't it?"

Not wishing to be involved, he replied: "Well, to tell you t'truth, Ah'm a stranger i' these parts."

L.D.

A MUCH-USED FOOTPATH crossed the village churchyard. Late one night a drunken man staggered across and dropped behind a tombstone, where he fell asleep.

Early next morning, he heard footsteps. The baker was on his way to work. The awakened man cried out: "What time is it?" The baker ran like mad. He had never before heard the dead cry out!

J.A.

OVERHEARD in the local: An argument had arisen during a game of snooker as to whether two balls were touching.

"Tha' can see from 'ere, white 'uns touchin', but t' red 'un in't," said an old boy in the corner.

A.T.

TWO YOUNG MEN tramping the Yorkshire Dales called at a country inn and arranged with the landlord to stay for bed and breakfast. They enquired whether he had any games other than darts.

"Mine host" mentioned an old billiards table upstairs. It was rarely used and, indeed, he could not remember when it was last played upon. He got the key and accompanied the visitors upstairs, opening the door, switching on the lights and removing the cover.

The landlord gave the young men a door key, observing: "When you have finished, cover the table and lock the door." They played a number of games of billiards and snooker before locking up and retiring to bed. The next morning, at breakfast, they returned the key and expressed their appreciation.

Two years later, the young men were in that area again. They called at the same inn, and in the course of conversation with the landlord mentioned their previous visit. Did the landlord remember them?

He replied: "Aye, I went up to the billiards room yesterday, to dust around. You'd left the lights on!"

H.J.

"A GIN AND TONIC, please," was my order in a Dales pub. "Bit o' lemon?" asked the landlord. "No, a gin with tonic, not bitter lemon," I replied. "Do you want a bit o' lemon with it?" repeated the landlord, showing me a slice of fresh lemon.

C.B.

IN A PUBLIC house in Swaledale at Whitsuntide, a visitor was laying down the law about the lack of entertainment in rural areas. He thought dalesfolk a "queer" lot and ended by asking one old chap what he did all winter.

The old chap looked thoughtful, and then said: "Well, after t' day's work we make up a good fire – and then we talk about all t' queer folk who've been here during t' summer."

H.W.

Yorkshire Speyks

MY HUSBAND (a Bristolian) and I were staying with my mother in Wensleydale. On Sunday we were attending the chapel anniversary.
"Who is to be the preacher?" asked my husband.
"Oh," said Mother, "we always have a man from off."
"A man from off?" my husband said enquiringly. "I didn't know there was a place called Off anywhere round here."
He's never lived it down.

K.M. Wright

DIALECT will persist. A small boy was taken for a bus ride. The bus crossed a river bridge.
"Look, Mummy – there's a waterfall!" he exclaimed.
"Weir, dear," gently reproved his mother.
"Theer!" the little lad replied.

K.L.

"... you tweet when you're twoten to."

A TEACHER WAS reading from the Scripture, "Blessed are they that mourn..." and interjected, "What is it to mourn, Johnny?"

"Wen's'day," Johnny replied brightly.

S.D.

AS A BOY, I had a pal who lived at Bolton, near Bradford. One Saturday afternoon when visiting him, his grandad came in, obviously distressed.

When asked the cause of his trouble, he told us that as he was suffering from flatulence, he had put his packet of Moorland's indigestion tablets in his "mac" pocket. While out walking, he had put his hand into his pocket to get his handkerchief, pulled it out, and with it his tablets.

Grandad continued: "Theer wor mi Moorlands sprodden aht all ower t'rooad up i' Eccisill (Eccleshill)!"

The poor old gentleman couldn't understand why we all fell about, laughing our heads off!

Joe Shortland

MY COUSIN was looking for somewhere to camp above Hunmanby, near Scarborough. A promising pitch was a nearby field and, seeing two small boys, he enquired whose field it was.

"Yon's Mosey's field," said the elder.

The little boy, aged about five, added dreamily: "Mosey's was the feller in t'Bible who saw t'bonnin' bush, and God said, "Moses, tek yer beeuts off – yon's holy ground where yer stannin'."

E.M. Salisbury

THIS HAPPENED in York many years ago. I was standing with a middle-aged acquaintance watching a bricklayer finishing the top of a new four-foot garden wall.

With a craftsman's pride in his job he was making a cement top, half round in shape. With a trowel and float he was intent upon a fine smooth finish.

We watched silently for at least five minutes when my companion suddenly shouted: "Oi!"

The builder looked up and said: "Wot?"

My companion then said: "Thoo'll 'ave t'blinking bods (birds) slippin' off theer!"

Then he quietly walked away.

B.W.